NORTH AMERICAN ANIMALS

American Badgers

by Rebecca Sabelko

BLASTOFF! READERS

3

BELLWETHER MEDIA • MINNEAPOLIS, MN

Note to Librarians, Teachers, and Parents:

Blastoff! Readers are carefully developed by literacy experts and combine standards-based content with developmentally appropriate text.

Level 1 provides the most support through repetition of high-frequency words, light text, predictable sentence patterns, and strong visual support.

Level 2 offers early readers a bit more challenge through varied simple sentences, increased text load, and less repetition of high-frequency words.

Level 3 advances early-fluent readers toward fluency through increased text and concept load, less reliance on visuals, longer sentences, and more literary language.

Level 4 builds reading stamina by providing more text per page, increased use of punctuation, greater variation in sentence patterns, and increasingly challenging vocabulary.

Level 5 encourages children to move from "learning to read" to "reading to learn" by providing even more text, varied writing styles, and less familiar topics.

Whichever book is right for your reader, Blastoff! Readers are the perfect books to build confidence and encourage a love of reading that will last a lifetime!

This edition first published in 2019 by Bellwether Media, Inc.

No part of this publication may be reproduced in whole or in part without written permission of the publisher. For information regarding permission, write to Bellwether Media, Inc., Attention: Permissions Department, 6012 Blue Circle Drive, Minnetonka, MN 55343.

Library of Congress Cataloging-in-Publication Data

Names: Sabelko, Rebecca, author.
Title: American Badgers / by Rebecca Sabelko.
Description: Minneapolis, MN : Bellwether Media, Inc., [2019] | Series: Blastoff! Readers. North American Animals | Audience: Ages 5-8. | Audience: K to grade 3. | Includes bibliographical references and index.
Identifiers: LCCN 2017056259 (print) | LCCN 2018004964 (ebook) | ISBN 9781626177956 (hardcover ; alk. paper) | ISBN 9781681035208 (ebook)
Subjects: LCSH: American badger–Juvenile literature. | Badgers–Juvenile literature.
Classification: LCC QL737.C25 (ebook) | LCC QL737.C25 S2294 2019 (print) | DDC 599.76/7–dc23
LC record available at https://lccn.loc.gov/2017056259

Editor: Betsy Rathburn   Designer: Josh Brink

Printed in the United States of America, North Mankato, MN.

Table of Contents

What Are American Badgers?

American badgers are **solitary** animals that like to rest. In the winter, they can sleep for 29 hours straight!

In the Wild

N

W E

S

American badger range = ▢

conservation status: least concern

Extinct

Extinct in the Wild

Critically Endangered

Endangered

Vulnerable

Near Threatened

Least Concern

Each summer, these **mammals** prowl much of the United States. They are also found in parts of Canada and Mexico.

Dry grasslands are American badgers' usual **habitat**. Hunting for **burrowing animals** is easier in open fields.

American badgers dig **dens** deep in the ground. These include many tunnels and a large room for sleeping.

claws

American badgers are powerful diggers. **Muscular** legs and long claws help them dig quickly.

Three eyelids keep their eyes safe while digging. Their cone-shaped heads make moving underground easy.

9

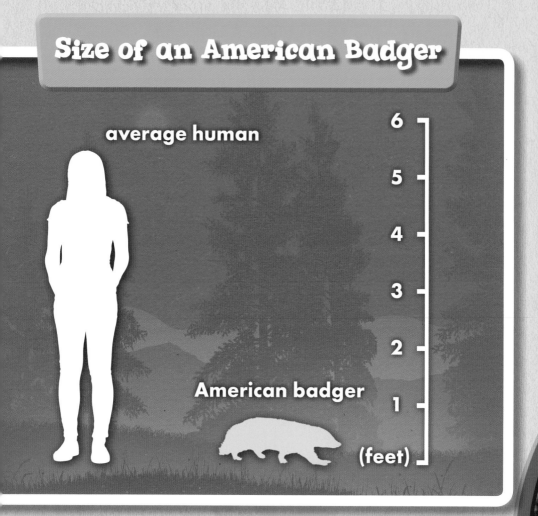

Size of an American Badger

average human

American badger

6
5
4
3
2
1
(feet)

Living underground means a short height is important. These badgers only stand 9 inches (23 centimeters) tall!

They can grow up to
3 feet (1 meter) long.

American badgers have grayish fur. Their faces are dark with a white stripe running from their noses to their backs.

Identify an American Badger

short legs

cone-shaped head

long, heavy claws

Badgers have **scent glands** near their tails. These give off a stinky smell that warns others to stay away!

American badgers can smell **prey** hiding underground. They use their mighty claws to dig straight for the animal. Then, they attack!

prairie dogs

pocket gophers

deer mice

American grasshoppers

bank swallows

prairie rattlesnakes

These **carnivores** bury large meals. They store the food in **caches** to eat later. The cool ground keeps meat fresh!

When American badgers meet **predators**, they often fight back! Claws and teeth protect the badgers from harm.

Sometimes, American badgers escape underground. Enemies have a hard time getting past their **defenses**!

Cozy Kits

Female badgers have up to five **kits** in spring. Kits are born blind and have very little fur.

These baby badgers **nurse** for up to three months. Grass-lined dens keep them safe and warm.

Kits learn to hunt and dig outside the den six weeks after birth. Soon, the kits are ready to be on their own. They search the grasslands for a new home!

Baby Facts

Name for babies:	kits
Size of litter:	1 to 5 kits
Length of pregnancy:	about 6 weeks
Time spent with mom:	5 to 6 months

Glossary

burrowing animals—animals that live in holes or tunnels underground

caches—hiding or storage places below ground

carnivores—animals that only eat meat

defenses—ways of keeping an animal safe

dens—sheltered places

habitat—lands with certain types of plants, animals, and weather

kits—baby badgers

mammals—warm-blooded animals that have backbones and feed their young milk

muscular—strong

nurse—to drink mom's milk

predators—animals that hunt other animals for food

prey—animals that are hunted by other animals for food

scent glands—special organs in the body that let out smells

solitary—living alone

To Learn More

AT THE LIBRARY
Heos, Bridget. *Do You Really Want to Meet a Badger*? Mankato, Minn.: Amicus High Interest Amicus Ink, 2017.

Niver, Heather Moore. *Badgers After Dark*. New York, N.Y.: Enslow Publishing, 2016.

Rathburn, Betsy. *Wolverines*. Minneapolis, Minn.: Bellwether Media, 2018.

ON THE WEB
Learning more about American badgers is as easy as 1, 2, 3.

1. Go to www.factsurfer.com.

2. Enter "American badgers" into the search box.

3. Click the "Surf" button and you will see a list of related web sites.

With factsurfer.com, finding more information is just a click away.

Index

The images in this book are reproduced through the courtesy of: Vertyr, front cover; Makhnach_S, front cover; Bill Peaslee, front cover; CGforStock, front cover; Action Sports Photography, p. 4; Matt Knoth, p. 6; Holly Kuchera, pp. 7, 12; Warren Metcalf, pp. 8, 13 (top left, bottom); Max Allen, p. 9; Kevin Wells Photography, pp. 10, 11; moosehenderson, p. 13 (top middle); Hart_Walter, p. 13 (top right); Andrew Kandel/ Alamy, p. 14; Gerald A. DeBoer, p. 15 (top left); Peter Graham/ Alamy, p. 15 (top right); Close Encounters Photo, p. 15 (middle left); LSAB Photography, p. 15 (middle right); Paul Reeves Photography, p. 15 (bottom left); Kerry Hargrove, p. 15 (bottom right); Imagesource, p. 16; Morales/ Age Fotostock/ SuperStock, p. 17; franzfoto.com/ Alamy, pp. 18-19; Dan Sullivan/ Alamy, p. 20; Randy Hume, p. 21.